ALL ABOUT YOU...

ABOUT ME: Write down the things I like, What mak

GOALS: What are my goals... What motivates me?

WHY? Write down why I want to make changes in my life!

PLAN: Have something to look forward to! My plans are:

RELAX: What shall I be doing to relax and unwind?

EXERCISE: What exercises will I be doing to speed things up?

MEASUREMENTS TRACKER

When measuring yourself with the measuring tape, the tape should fit snugly against the surface of your skin. It should not press into the skin at any point. When wrapped around you, the measuring tape should be parallel with the floor, and not askew. When measuring your bust/chest, you'll get the best results if both arms are at your side. You may need assistance for this!

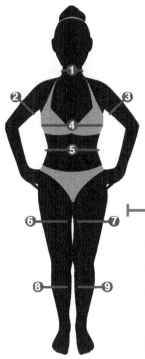

Getting the same result, does not mean you haven't lost any weight.
Remember your measurements are only guide lines.
Measure yourself today, (**Week 1**), then weeks 3, 5, 7, 9 & 10

MEASUREMENTS   WEEKS

1	2	3	4	5	6	7	8	9	
									1
									3
									5
									7
									9
									10

WEIGHT TRACKER GRAPH

Enter your "**Stone**" Weight only in **Box A** - then mark on the graph your "**Pound**" Weight!

HOW MUCH AND HOW FAST?

You are looking to lose a healthy 1 to 1 and a half pound per week. Any more than this and your body may go into starvation mode. You want to avoid this at all costs because this may result in failure, or your weight coming back super fast as soon as your diet cycle ends. To avoid this and ensure success go to our help page for more information and how to avoid this situation. "Success is yours with a little knowledge "

Visit: fitnesswow.co.uk

From the Home Page, select "More" then "Online extra content" - Find 10 Weeks to Wow!

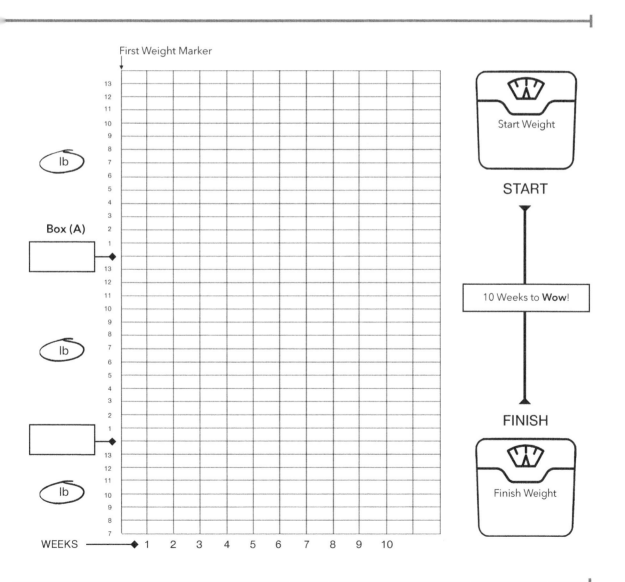

TICKS AND BEVERAGES

Your beverages are just as important as your meals. Lots of people who are on a diet forget that beverages contain Calories. Some people drink more beverages than others. Sometimes this may be a work environment factor or simply drinking becomes a habit rather than a need.

"Counting ticks is like counting Calories"

If we all took in fluids for our needs only, we would only drink water. This would be a good thing, but we don't simply drink to nourish and hydrate our bodies anymore, we drink for flavour, enjoyment and to socialise.

Beverages taste nice and supply us with a little boost or kick we are looking for.
The most common beverages are, you guessed it, tea, coffee and hot chocolate.

+ 1 Sugar = 30 Calories x 10 Cups = 300 Calories

The reason you need to place a tick on your Diary page each time you have a beverage, is so you can see at a glance how many beverages you are having!

You may be shocked at the amount you do have. Reducing your beverages alone may be all the difference you're looking for to lose weight.

Simply looking at the number of ticks on your page may give you a true picture to whether you are just having too many, or too many in one particular part of the day. You may be able to say to yourself - NO more coffees in the morning, or I will at least reduce this by half!

If you take sugar with your Tea & Coffee, we have a clever little way for you to reduce this by half, or to nothing without you evening noticing it. Visit our website for more information.

YOUR FITNESSWOW EXERCISE PLAN

Exercising is optional, but advised... It's easier to burn Calories off than starve them off! This is a simple exercise formula and has be designed to cater for all levels of fitness, stamina and flexibility, it works brilliantly because you get to choose the exercises that are right for you and your body type.

Perform your exercises and tick completed on your planner page to keep a record of your progress throughout the forthcoming weeks.

This exercise programme is - Timed Exercise and Timed Resting. Perform your exercises for **60 Seconds** and rest for **60 Seconds**. To increase the intensity of your routine, you can reduce your resting times by **15 to 30 Seconds**.

Perform your chosen exercises for **60 Seconds** and Rest / Pause for **60 Seconds**. Repeat each exercise **3 times in a row**. Tick when completed so you can track your performance.

Low Level Intensity

✔ Chair Squats
✔ The Bridge
✔ Quater Squats
✔ The Plank

Medium Level Intensity

✔ Air Punches
✔ Free Squats
✔ Lunges
✔ Stair Walking

High Level Intensity

✔ Jumping Jacks
✔ Burpees
✔ Mountain Climbers
✔ Walking Lunges

An illustration and instruction for each exercise can be found on our website: www.weightwow.co.uk   While you're visiting, check out our amazing weight loss exercise formulas for all levels of fitness and **Weight Loss Goals**. "Tab More"

From the Home Page select More, then:
Online Extra Content - then Select "**10 Weeks to Wow**"

Get yourself an amazing **FREE** Exercise Journal... Free Postage!

All you have to do is spare us 3 minutes of your time to review this book on amazon or post a picture on Instagram. For more information visit our website and hit the "More" Button...

DATE: / / Bed [:] Awake [:] Hours [ ]

NOTES

Today I am grateful for:

TO DO

☐
☐
☐
☐
☐

MEAL PLANNER - Tomorrows Meals Organised!

TODAYS HEALTHY HABITS - Five a day - Colour me in - Water - Fruit & Veggies

ACTIVITY

Total Steps [ ]

Total Floors / Flights [ ]

EXERCISE

Completed Exercise Routine

3 x 1 Min / Exercise 1 ☐ ☐ ☐

3 x 1 Min / Exercise 2 ☐ ☐ ☐

3 x 1 Min / Exercise 3 ☐ ☐ ☐

Points Total

[ ] (A) + (B) + (C) ◄

Beverage Total

[ ] ☑

Feeling / Mood Emojis

☺ 😐 😮 ☹

BREAKFAST / MORNING

Points ✓

LUNCH / AFTERNOON

✓

DINNER / EVENING

✓

Morning: Points

A

Afternoon: Points

B

Evening: Points

C

DATE: / / Bed [:] Awake [:] Hours [ ]

NOTES

TO DO

☐
☐
☐
☐

Today I am grateful for:

☐

MEAL PLANNER - Tomorrows Meals Organised!

TODAYS HEALTHY HABITS - Five a day - Colour me in - Water - Fruit & Veggies

ACTIVITY

Total Steps [ ]

Total Floors / Flights [ ]

EXERCISE

Completed Exercise Routine

3 x 1 Min / Exercise 1 ☐ ☐ ☐

3 x 1 Min / Exercise 2 ☐ ☐ ☐

3 x 1 Min / Exercise 3 ☐ ☐ ☐

Points Total

[ ] (A) + (B) + (C) ◄

Beverage Total

[ ]

Feeling / Mood Emojis

🙂 😐 😮 🙁

BREAKFAST / MORNING

Points ✓

LUNCH / AFTERNOON

✓

DINNER / EVENING

✓

Morning: Points   Afternoon: Points   Evening: Points

A   B   C

DATE: /   /   Bed [:]   Awake [:]   Hours [   ]

NOTES

TO DO

☐
☐
☐
☐
☐

Today I am grateful for:

MEAL PLANNER - Tomorrows Meals Organised!

TODAYS HEALTHY HABITS - Five a day - Colour me in - Water - Fruit & Veggies

ACTIVITY

Total Steps [   ]

Total Floors / Flights [   ]

EXERCISE

Completed Exercise Routine

3 x 1 Min / Exercise 1   ☐ ☐ ☐

3 x 1 Min / Exercise 2   ☐ ☐ ☐

3 x 1 Min / Exercise 3   ☐ ☐ ☐

Points Total

[   ]   (A) + (B) + (C) ◄

Beverage Total

[   ]   ☑ ◄

Feeling / Mood Emojis

🙂 😐 😮 🙁

BREAKFAST / MORNING

Points ✓

LUNCH / AFTERNOON

✓

DINNER / EVENING

✓

Morning: Points   Afternoon: Points   Evening: Points

A   B   C

DATE: / / Bed [:] Awake [:] Hours [ ]

NOTES

....

....

....

....

Today I am grateful for:
....

TO DO

- [ ]
- [ ]
- [ ]
- [ ]
- [ ]

MEAL PLANNER - Tomorrows Meals Organised!

....

....

....

....

....

TODAYS HEALTHY HABITS - Five a day - Colour me in - Water - Fruit & Veggies

ACTIVITY

Total Steps [ ]

Total Floors / Flights [ ]

EXERCISE

Completed Exercise Routine

3 x 1 Min / Exercise 1 [ ] [ ] [ ]

3 x 1 Min / Exercise 2 [ ] [ ] [ ]

3 x 1 Min / Exercise 3 [ ] [ ] [ ]

Points Total

[ ] (A) + (B) + (C) ◄

Beverage Total

[ ]

Feeling / Mood Emojis

:) :| :O :(

BREAKFAST / MORNING

Points ✓

LUNCH / AFTERNOON

✓

DINNER / EVENING

✓

Morning: Points

A

Afternoon: Points

B

Evening: Points

C

DATE: /   /   Bed [:]   Awake [:]   Hours [ ]

NOTES

....
....
....
....
....
Today I am grateful for:

TO DO

☐
☐
☐
☐
☐

MEAL PLANNER - Tomorrows Meals Organised!

....
....
....
....
....

TODAYS HEALTHY HABITS - Five a day - Colour me in - Water - Fruit & Veggies

ACTIVITY

Total Steps [ ]

Total Floors / Flights [ ]

EXERCISE

Completed Exercise Routine

3 x 1 Min / Exercise 1 ☐ ☐ ☐

3 x 1 Min / Exercise 2 ☐ ☐ ☐

3 x 1 Min / Exercise 3 ☐ ☐ ☐

Points Total

[ ] (A) + (B) + (C) ◄

Beverage Total

[ ] ☑

Feeling / Mood Emojis

😊 😐 😲 ☹

BREAKFAST / MORNING

Points ✓

LUNCH / AFTERNOON

✓

DINNER / EVENING

✓

Morning: Points

Afternoon: Points

Evening: Points

A

B

C

DATE: / / Bed [:] Awake [:] Hours [ ]

NOTES

....
....
....
....

Today I am grateful for:
....

TO DO

☐
☐
☐
☐
☐

MEAL PLANNER - Tomorrows Meals Organised!

....
....
....
....
....
....

TODAYS HEALTHY HABITS - Five a day - Colour me in - Water - Fruit & Veggies

ACTIVITY

Total Steps [ ]

Total Floors / Flights [ ]

EXERCISE

Completed Exercise Routine

3 x 1 Min / Exercise 1 ☐ ☐ ☐

3 x 1 Min / Exercise 2 ☐ ☐ ☐

3 x 1 Min / Exercise 3 ☐ ☐ ☐

Points Total

[ ] (A) + (B) + (C) ◄

Beverage Total

[ ] ☑

Feeling / Mood Emojis

☺ 😐 😮 ☹

BREAKFAST / MORNING

Points ✓

LUNCH / AFTERNOON

✓

DINNER / EVENING

✓

Morning: Points

A

Afternoon: Points

B

Evening: Points

C

DATE: / / Bed : Awake : Hours

NOTES

Today I am grateful for:

TO DO

☐
☐
☐
☐
☐

MEAL PLANNER - Tomorrows Meals Organised!

TODAYS HEALTHY HABITS - Five a day - Colour me in - Water - Fruit & Veggies

ACTIVITY

Total Steps

Total Floors / Flights

EXERCISE

Completed Exercise Routine

3 x 1 Min / Exercise 1

3 x 1 Min / Exercise 2

3 x 1 Min / Exercise 3

Points Total

(A) + (B) + (C)

Beverage Total

Feeling / Mood Emojis

BREAKFAST / MORNING

Points ✓

LUNCH / AFTERNOON

✓

DINNER / EVENING

✓

Morning: Points

A

Afternoon: Points

B

Evening: Points

C

DATE: / / Bed [:] Awake [:] Hours [ ]

NOTES

TO DO
- [ ]
- [ ]
- [ ]
- [ ]
- [ ]

Today I am grateful for:

MEAL PLANNER - Tomorrows Meals Organised!

TODAYS HEALTHY HABITS - Five a day - Colour me in - Water - Fruit & Veggies

ACTIVITY

Total Steps [ ]

Total Floors / Flights [ ]

EXERCISE

Completed Exercise Routine

3 x 1 Min / Exercise 1 [ ] [ ] [ ]

3 x 1 Min / Exercise 2 [ ] [ ] [ ]

3 x 1 Min / Exercise 3 [ ] [ ] [ ]

Points Total

[ ] (A) + (B) + (C) ◄

Beverage Total

[ ] ☑

Feeling / Mood Emojis

☺ 😐 😮 ☹

BREAKFAST / MORNING

Points ✓

LUNCH / AFTERNOON

✓

DINNER / EVENING

✓

Morning: Points   Afternoon: Points   Evening: Points

A   B   C

✓

DATE: / / Bed [:] Awake [:] Hours [ ]

NOTES

TO DO
- [ ]
- [ ]
- [ ]
- [ ]
- [ ]

Today I am grateful for:

MEAL PLANNER - Tomorrows Meals Organised!

TODAYS HEALTHY HABITS - Five a day - Colour me in - Water - Fruit & Veggies

ACTIVITY

Total Steps [ ]

Total Floors / Flights [ ]

EXERCISE

Completed Exercise Routine

3 x 1 Min / Exercise 1 [ ] [ ] [ ]

3 x 1 Min / Exercise 2 [ ] [ ] [ ]

3 x 1 Min / Exercise 3 [ ] [ ] [ ]

Points Total

[ ] (A) + (B) + (C) ◄

Beverage Total

[ ]

Feeling / Mood Emojis

☺ 😐 😮 ☹

BREAKFAST / MORNING

Points

LUNCH / AFTERNOON

DINNER / EVENING

Morning: Points

Afternoon: Points

Evening: Points

A

B

C

DATE: / / Bed [:] Awake [:] Hours [ ]

NOTES

....
....
....
....
....

Today I am grateful for:

TO DO

- [ ]
- [ ]
- [ ]
- [ ]
- [ ]

MEAL PLANNER - Tomorrows Meals Organised!

....
....
....
....
....

TODAYS HEALTHY HABITS - Five a day - Colour me in - Water - Fruit & Veggies

ACTIVITY

Total Steps [ ]

Total Floors / Flights [ ]

EXERCISE

Completed Exercise Routine

3 x 1 Min / Exercise 1 [ ] [ ] [ ]

3 x 1 Min / Exercise 2 [ ] [ ] [ ]

3 x 1 Min / Exercise 3 [ ] [ ] [ ]

Points Total

[ ] (A) + (B) + (C) ◀

Beverage Total

[ ]

Feeling / Mood Emojis

BREAKFAST / MORNING

Points ✔

LUNCH / AFTERNOON

✔

DINNER / EVENING

✔

Morning: Points   Afternoon: Points   Evening: Points

● A [   ]   B [   ]   C [   ]

DATE: / / Bed [:] Awake [:] Hours [ ]

NOTES

....
....
....
....
Today I am grateful for:
....

TO DO

☐
☐
☐
☐
☐

MEAL PLANNER - Tomorrows Meals Organised!

....
....
....
....
....
....

TODAYS HEALTHY HABITS - Five a day - Colour me in - Water - Fruit & Veggies

ACTIVITY

Total Steps [ ]

Total Floors / Flights [ ]

EXERCISE

Completed Exercise Routine

3 x 1 Min / Exercise 1   ☐ ☐ ☐

3 x 1 Min / Exercise 2   ☐ ☐ ☐

3 x 1 Min / Exercise 3   ☐ ☐ ☐

Points Total

[ ]   (A) + (B) + (C) ◄

Beverage Total

[ ]

Feeling / Mood Emojis

☺ 😐 😮 ☹

BREAKFAST / MORNING

Points ✓

LUNCH / AFTERNOON

✓

DINNER / EVENING

✓

Morning: Points

Afternoon: Points

Evening: Points

A **B** **C**

DATE: /   /   Bed [:]   Awake [:]   Hours [   ]

NOTES

....

....

....

....

Today I am grateful for:

....

TO DO

☐
☐
☐
☐
☐

MEAL PLANNER - Tomorrows Meals Organised!

....

....

....

....

....

TODAYS HEALTHY HABITS - Five a day - Colour me in - Water - Fruit & Veggies

ACTIVITY

Total Steps [   ]

Total Floors / Flights [   ]

EXERCISE

Completed Exercise Routine

3 x 1 Min / Exercise 1 ☐ ☐ ☐

3 x 1 Min / Exercise 2 ☐ ☐ ☐

3 x 1 Min / Exercise 3 ☐ ☐ ☐

Points Total

[   ]   (A) + (B) + (C) ◄

Beverage Total

[   ]   ☑

Feeling / Mood Emojis

☺ 😐 😮 ☹

BREAKFAST / MORNING

Points

LUNCH / AFTERNOON

DINNER / EVENING

Morning: Points   Afternoon: Points   Evening: Points

A   **B**   **C**

DATE: /   /   Bed [:]   Awake [:]   Hours [ ]

NOTES

....
....
....
....

Today I am grateful for:

TO DO

☐
☐
☐
☐
☐

MEAL PLANNER - Tomorrows Meals Organised!

....
....
....
....

TODAYS HEALTHY HABITS - Five a day - Colour me in - Water - Fruit & Veggies

ACTIVITY

Total Steps [ ]

Total Floors / Flights [ ]

EXERCISE

Completed Exercise Routine

3 x 1 Min / Exercise 1   ☐ ☐ ☐

3 x 1 Min / Exercise 2   ☐ ☐ ☐

3 x 1 Min / Exercise 3   ☐ ☐ ☐

Points Total

[ ]   (A) + (B) + (C)

Beverage Total

[ ]   ☑

Feeling / Mood Emojis

🙂 😐 😮 🙁

BREAKFAST / MORNING

Points ✓

LUNCH / AFTERNOON

✓

DINNER / EVENING

✓

Morning: Points

Afternoon: Points

Evening: Points

A

B

C

DATE: / / Bed ☐ : ☐ Awake ☐ : ☐ Hours ☐

NOTES

TO DO
- ☐
- ☐
- ☐
- ☐
- ☐

Today I am grateful for:

MEAL PLANNER - Tomorrows Meals Organised!

TODAYS HEALTHY HABITS - Five a day - Colour me in - Water - Fruit & Veggies

ACTIVITY

Total Steps ☐

Total Floors / Flights ☐

EXERCISE

Completed Exercise Routine

3 x 1 Min / Exercise 1 ☐ ☐ ☐

3 x 1 Min / Exercise 2 ☐ ☐ ☐

3 x 1 Min / Exercise 3 ☐ ☐ ☐

Points Total

☐ (A) + (B) + (C) ←

Beverage Total

☐ ☑

Feeling / Mood Emojis

☺ 😐 😲 ☹

BREAKFAST / MORNING

Points ✔

LUNCH / AFTERNOON

✔

DINNER / EVENING

✔

Morning: Points

A

Afternoon: Points

B

Evening: Points

C

DATE: / / Bed : Awake : Hours

NOTES

Today I am grateful for:

TO DO

☐
☐
☐
☐
☐

MEAL PLANNER - Tomorrows Meals Organised!

TODAYS HEALTHY HABITS - Five a day - Colour me in - Water - Fruit & Veggies

ACTIVITY

Total Steps

Total Floors / Flights

EXERCISE

Completed Exercise Routine

3 x 1 Min / Exercise 1

3 x 1 Min / Exercise 2

3 x 1 Min / Exercise 3

Points Total

(A) + (B) + (C)

Beverage Total

Feeling / Mood Emojis

BREAKFAST / MORNING

Points ✓

LUNCH / AFTERNOON

✓

DINNER / EVENING

✓

Morning: Points

Afternoon: Points

Evening: Points

A

B

C

DATE: / /   Bed [:]   Awake [:]   Hours [ ]

NOTES

TO DO

☐
☐
☐
☐
Today I am grateful for: ☐

MEAL PLANNER - Tomorrows Meals Organised!

TODAYS HEALTHY HABITS - Five a day - Colour me in - Water - Fruit & Veggies

ACTIVITY

Total Steps [ ]

Total Floors / Flights [ ]

EXERCISE

Completed Exercise Routine

3 x 1 Min / Exercise 1   ☐ ☐ ☐

3 x 1 Min / Exercise 2   ☐ ☐ ☐

3 x 1 Min / Exercise 3   ☐ ☐ ☐

Points Total

[ ]   (A) + (B) + (C) ◄

Beverage Total

[ ]   ☑

Feeling / Mood Emojis

🙂 😐 😮 🙁

BREAKFAST / MORNING

Points ✓

LUNCH / AFTERNOON

✓

DINNER / EVENING

✓

Morning: Points

Afternoon: Points

Evening: Points

A

B

C

DATE: / /   Bed [:]   Awake [:]   Hours [ ]

NOTES

Today I am grateful for:

TO DO

☐
☐
☐
☐
☐

MEAL PLANNER - Tomorrows Meals Organised!

TODAYS HEALTHY HABITS - Five a day - Colour me in - Water - Fruit & Veggies

ACTIVITY

Total Steps [ ]

Total Floors / Flights [ ]

EXERCISE

Completed Exercise Routine

3 x 1 Min / Exercise 1 ☐ ☐ ☐

3 x 1 Min / Exercise 2 ☐ ☐ ☐

3 x 1 Min / Exercise 3 ☐ ☐ ☐

Points Total

[ ] (A) + (B) + (C) ◀

Beverage Total

[ ] ☑

Feeling / Mood Emojis

☺ 😐 😮 ☹

BREAKFAST / MORNING

Points ✓

LUNCH / AFTERNOON

✓

DINNER / EVENING

✓

Morning: Points

A

Afternoon: Points

B

Evening: Points

C

DATE: / /   Bed [:]   Awake [:]   Hours [ ]

NOTES

....
....
....
....

Today I am grateful for:

TO DO

.... ☐
.... ☐
.... ☐
.... ☐
.... ☐

MEAL PLANNER - Tomorrows Meals Organised!

....
....
....
....

TODAYS HEALTHY HABITS - Five a day - Colour me in - Water - Fruit & Veggies

ACTIVITY

Total Steps [ ]

Total Floors / Flights [ ]

EXERCISE

Completed Exercise Routine

3 x 1 Min / Exercise 1 ☐ ☐ ☐

3 x 1 Min / Exercise 2 ☐ ☐ ☐

3 x 1 Min / Exercise 3 ☐ ☐ ☐

Points Total

[ ]   (A) + (B) + (C) ◄

Beverage Total

[ ]   ☑

Feeling / Mood Emojis

☺ 😐 😧 ☹

BREAKFAST / MORNING

Points ✓

LUNCH / AFTERNOON

✓

DINNER / EVENING

✓

Morning: Points	Afternoon: Points	Evening: Points
A	B	C

DATE: / / Bed [:] Awake [:] Hours [ ]

NOTES

TO DO
- [ ]
- [ ]
- [ ]
- [ ]
- [ ]

Today I am grateful for:

MEAL PLANNER - Tomorrows Meals Organised!

TODAYS HEALTHY HABITS - Five a day - Colour me in - Water - Fruit & Veggies

ACTIVITY

Total Steps [ ]

Total Floors / Flights [ ]

Points Total

[ ] (A) + (B) + (C) ◄

Beverage Total

[ ] ☑

EXERCISE ──────────

Completed Exercise Routine

3 x 1 Min / Exercise 1 [ ] [ ] [ ]

3 x 1 Min / Exercise 2 [ ] [ ] [ ]

3 x 1 Min / Exercise 3 [ ] [ ] [ ]

Feeling / Mood Emojis

🙂 😐 😮 🙁

BREAKFAST / MORNING

Points ✔

LUNCH / AFTERNOON

✔

DINNER / EVENING

✔

Morning: Points   Afternoon: Points   Evening: Points

A [   ]   B [   ]   C [   ]

DATE: / / Bed ☐ : ☐ Awake ☐ : ☐ Hours ☐

NOTES

Today I am grateful for:

TO DO

☐
☐
☐
☐
☐

MEAL PLANNER - Tomorrows Meals Organised!

TODAYS HEALTHY HABITS - Five a day - Colour me in - Water - Fruit & Veggies

ACTIVITY

Total Steps ☐

Total Floors / Flights ☐

EXERCISE

Completed Exercise Routine

3 x 1 Min / Exercise 1 ☐ ☐ ☐

3 x 1 Min / Exercise 2 ☐ ☐ ☐

3 x 1 Min / Exercise 3 ☐ ☐ ☐

Points Total

☐ (A) + (B) + (C) ◄

Beverage Total

☐ ☑

Feeling / Mood Emojis

☺ 😐 😮 ☹

BREAKFAST / MORNING

	Points	✓

LUNCH / AFTERNOON

	Points	✓

DINNER / EVENING

	Points	✓

Morning: Points

A

Afternoon: Points

B

Evening: Points

C

DATE: /   /   Bed [:]   Awake [:]   Hours [ ]

NOTES

TO DO

☐
☐
☐
☐

Today I am grateful for:

☐

MEAL PLANNER - Tomorrows Meals Organised!

TODAYS HEALTHY HABITS - Five a day - Colour me in - Water - Fruit & Veggies

ACTIVITY

Total Steps [ ]

Total Floors / Flights [ ]

EXERCISE

Completed Exercise Routine

3 x 1 Min / Exercise 1   ☐ ☐ ☐

3 x 1 Min / Exercise 2   ☐ ☐ ☐

3 x 1 Min / Exercise 3   ☐ ☐ ☐

Points Total

[ ]   (A) + (B) + (C) ◄

Beverage Total

[ ]

Feeling / Mood Emojis

🙂 😐 😮 🙁

BREAKFAST / MORNING

Points ✓

LUNCH / AFTERNOON

✓

DINNER / EVENING

✓

Morning: Points   Afternoon: Points   Evening: Points

A   **B**   **C**

DATE: / / Bed ☐ : ☐ Awake ☐ : ☐ Hours ☐

NOTES

TO DO

☐
☐
☐
☐
☐

Today I am grateful for:

MEAL PLANNER - Tomorrows Meals Organised!

TODAYS HEALTHY HABITS - Five a day - Colour me in - Water - Fruit & Veggies

ACTIVITY

Total Steps ☐

Total Floors / Flights ☐

EXERCISE

Completed Exercise Routine

3 x 1 Min / Exercise 1 ☐ ☐ ☐

3 x 1 Min / Exercise 2 ☐ ☐ ☐

3 x 1 Min / Exercise 3 ☐ ☐ ☐

Points Total

☐ (A) + (B) + (C) ◄

Beverage Total

☐ ☑

Feeling / Mood Emojis

☺ 😐 😲 ☹

BREAKFAST / MORNING

Points ✓

LUNCH / AFTERNOON

✓

DINNER / EVENING

✓

Morning: Points   Afternoon: Points   Evening: Points

A [   ]   **B** [   ]   **C** [   ]

DATE: / / Bed [:] Awake [:] Hours [ ]

NOTES

TO DO

- [ ]
- [ ]
- [ ]
- [ ]
- [ ]

Today I am grateful for:

MEAL PLANNER - Tomorrows Meals Organised!

TODAYS HEALTHY HABITS - Five a day - Colour me in - Water - Fruit & Veggies

ACTIVITY

Total Steps [ ]

Total Floors / Flights [ ]

EXERCISE

Completed Exercise Routine

3 x 1 Min / Exercise 1 [ ] [ ] [ ]

3 x 1 Min / Exercise 2 [ ] [ ] [ ]

3 x 1 Min / Exercise 3 [ ] [ ] [ ]

Points Total

[ ] (A) + (B) + (C) ◄

Beverage Total

[ ] ◄

Feeling / Mood Emojis

BREAKFAST / MORNING

Points ✓

LUNCH / AFTERNOON

✓

DINNER / EVENING

✓

Morning: Points

A

Afternoon: Points

B

Evening: Points

C

DATE: / / Bed [:] Awake [:] Hours [ ]

NOTES

....
....
....
....
....

Today I am grateful for:
....

TO DO

☐
☐
☐
☐
☐

MEAL PLANNER - Tomorrows Meals Organised!

....
....
....
....
....
....

TODAYS HEALTHY HABITS - Five a day - Colour me in - Water - Fruit & Veggies

ACTIVITY

Total Steps [ ]

Total Floors / Flights [ ]

EXERCISE

Completed Exercise Routine

3 x 1 Min / Exercise 1 ☐ ☐ ☐

3 x 1 Min / Exercise 2 ☐ ☐ ☐

3 x 1 Min / Exercise 3 ☐ ☐ ☐

Points Total

[ ] (A) + (B) + (C) ◄

Beverage Total

[ ] ☑

Feeling / Mood Emojis

☺ 😐 😮 ☹

BREAKFAST / MORNING

Points ✓

LUNCH / AFTERNOON

✓

DINNER / EVENING

✓

Morning: Points Afternoon: Points Evening: Points

A B C

DATE: /   /   Bed [:]   Awake [:]   Hours [ ]

NOTES

TO DO

☐
☐
☐
☐
☐

Today I am grateful for:

MEAL PLANNER - Tomorrows Meals Organised!

TODAYS HEALTHY HABITS - Five a day - Colour me in - Water - Fruit & Veggies

ACTIVITY

Total Steps [ ]

Total Floors / Flights [ ]

EXERCISE

Completed Exercise Routine

3 x 1 Min / Exercise 1 ☐ ☐ ☐

3 x 1 Min / Exercise 2 ☐ ☐ ☐

3 x 1 Min / Exercise 3 ☐ ☐ ☐

Points Total

[ ]   (A) + (B) + (C) ◄

Beverage Total

[ ]   ☑

Feeling / Mood Emojis

☺ 😐 😮 ☹

BREAKFAST / MORNING

Points ✓

LUNCH / AFTERNOON

✓

DINNER / EVENING

✓

Morning: Points	Afternoon: Points	Evening: Points
A	B	C

DATE: / / Bed [:] Awake [:] Hours [ ]

NOTES

....
....
....
....

Today I am grateful for:

TO DO

- [ ]
- [ ]
- [ ]
- [ ]
- [ ]

MEAL PLANNER - Tomorrows Meals Organised!

....
....
....
....
....

TODAYS HEALTHY HABITS - Five a day - Colour me in - Water - Fruit & Veggies

ACTIVITY

Total Steps [ ]

Total Floors / Flights [ ]

EXERCISE

Completed Exercise Routine

3 x 1 Min / Exercise 1

3 x 1 Min / Exercise 2

3 x 1 Min / Exercise 3

Points Total

[ ] (A) + (B) + (C) ◄

Beverage Total

[ ] ☑

Feeling / Mood Emojis

BREAKFAST / MORNING

Points ✓

LUNCH / AFTERNOON

✓

DINNER / EVENING

✓

Morning: Points	Afternoon: Points	Evening: Points
A	B	C

DATE: / / Bed [:] Awake [:] Hours [ ]

NOTES

TO DO

☐
☐
☐
☐

Today I am grateful for: ☐

MEAL PLANNER - Tomorrows Meals Organised!

TODAYS HEALTHY HABITS - Five a day - Colour me in - Water - Fruit & Veggies

ACTIVITY

Total Steps [ ]

Total Floors / Flights [ ]

EXERCISE

Completed Exercise Routine

3 x 1 Min / Exercise 1 ☐ ☐ ☐

3 x 1 Min / Exercise 2 ☐ ☐ ☐

3 x 1 Min / Exercise 3 ☐ ☐ ☐

Points Total

[ ] (A) + (B) + (C) ◄

Beverage Total

[ ] ☑

Feeling / Mood Emojis

🙂 😐 😮 🙁

BREAKFAST / MORNING

Points | ✓

LUNCH / AFTERNOON

✓

DINNER / EVENING

✓

Morning: Points	Afternoon: Points	Evening: Points
A	B	C

DATE: / / **Bed** [:] **Awake** [:] **Hours** [ ]

NOTES

Today I am grateful for:

TO DO

- [ ]
- [ ]
- [ ]
- [ ]
- [ ]

MEAL PLANNER - Tomorrows Meals Organised!

TODAYS HEALTHY HABITS - Five a day - Colour me in - Water - Fruit & Veggies

ACTIVITY

Total Steps [ ]

Total Floors / Flights [ ]

EXERCISE

Completed Exercise Routine

3 x 1 Min / Exercise 1 [ ] [ ] [ ]

3 x 1 Min / Exercise 2 [ ] [ ] [ ]

3 x 1 Min / Exercise 3 [ ] [ ] [ ]

Points Total

[ ] (A) + (B) + (C) ◄

Beverage Total

[ ] ✓

Feeling / Mood Emojis

☺ 😐 😮 ☹

BREAKFAST / MORNING

Points ✓

LUNCH / AFTERNOON

✓

DINNER / EVENING

✓

Morning: Points | Afternoon: Points | Evening: Points

A | B | C

DATE: / / Bed [:] Awake [:] Hours [ ]

NOTES

TO DO

- [ ]
- [ ]
- [ ]
- [ ]

Today I am grateful for:

- [ ]

MEAL PLANNER - Tomorrows Meals Organised!

TODAYS HEALTHY HABITS - Five a day - Colour me in - Water - Fruit & Veggies

ACTIVITY

Total Steps [ ]

Total Floors / Flights [ ]

EXERCISE

Completed Exercise Routine

3 x 1 Min / Exercise 1 [ ] [ ] [ ]

3 x 1 Min / Exercise 2 [ ] [ ] [ ]

3 x 1 Min / Exercise 3 [ ] [ ] [ ]

Points Total

[ ] (A) + (B) + (C) ◄

Beverage Total

[ ]

Feeling / Mood Emojis

BREAKFAST / MORNING

Points ✓

LUNCH / AFTERNOON

✓

DINNER / EVENING

✓

Morning: Points

A [ ]

Afternoon: Points

B [ ]

Evening: Points

C [ ]

DATE: / / Bed [:] Awake [:] Hours [ ]

NOTES

TO DO

☐
☐
☐
☐
☐

Today I am grateful for:

MEAL PLANNER - Tomorrows Meals Organised!

TODAYS HEALTHY HABITS - Five a day - Colour me in - Water - Fruit & Veggies

ACTIVITY

Total Steps [ ]

Total Floors / Flights [ ]

EXERCISE

Completed Exercise Routine

3 x 1 Min / Exercise 1 ☐ ☐ ☐

3 x 1 Min / Exercise 2 ☐ ☐ ☐

3 x 1 Min / Exercise 3 ☐ ☐ ☐

Points Total

[ ] (A) + (B) + (C) ◄

Beverage Total

[ ] ☑

Feeling / Mood Emojis

☺ 😐 😮 ☹

BREAKFAST / MORNING

Points ✓

LUNCH / AFTERNOON

✓

DINNER / EVENING

✓

Morning: Points

Afternoon: Points

Evening: Points

A **B** **C**

DATE: / / Bed [:] Awake [:] Hours [ ]

NOTES

TO DO

☐
☐
☐
☐
Today I am grateful for: ☐

MEAL PLANNER - Tomorrows Meals Organised!

TODAYS HEALTHY HABITS - Five a day - Colour me in - Water - Fruit & Veggies

ACTIVITY

Total Steps [ ]

Total Floors / Flights [ ]

EXERCISE

Completed Exercise Routine

3 x 1 Min / Exercise 1 ☐ ☐ ☐

3 x 1 Min / Exercise 2 ☐ ☐ ☐

3 x 1 Min / Exercise 3 ☐ ☐ ☐

Points Total

[ ] (A) + (B) + (C)

Beverage Total

[ ]

Feeling / Mood Emojis

BREAKFAST / MORNING

Points ✓

LUNCH / AFTERNOON

✓

DINNER / EVENING

✓

Morning: Points

Afternoon: Points

Evening: Points

A **B** **C**

DATE: / / Bed [:] Awake [:] Hours [ ]

NOTES

TO DO

☐
☐
☐
☐

Today I am grateful for:

☐

MEAL PLANNER - Tomorrows Meals Organised!

TODAYS HEALTHY HABITS - Five a day - Colour me in - Water - Fruit & Veggies

ACTIVITY

Total Steps [ ]

Total Floors / Flights [ ]

EXERCISE

Completed Exercise Routine

3 x 1 Min / Exercise 1 ☐ ☐ ☐

3 x 1 Min / Exercise 2 ☐ ☐ ☐

3 x 1 Min / Exercise 3 ☐ ☐ ☐

Points Total

[ ] (A) + (B) + (C) ◄

Beverage Total

[ ] ☑

Feeling / Mood Emojis

☺ 😐 😮 ☹

BREAKFAST / MORNING

Points ✓

LUNCH / AFTERNOON

✓

DINNER / EVENING

✓

Morning: Points	Afternoon: Points	Evening: Points
A	B	C

DATE: / / **Bed** [:] **Awake** [:] **Hours** [ ]

NOTES

TO DO

☐
☐
☐
☐

Today I am grateful for:

☐

MEAL PLANNER - Tomorrows Meals Organised!

TODAYS HEALTHY HABITS - Five a day - Colour me in - Water - Fruit & Veggies

ACTIVITY

Total Steps [ ]

Total Floors / Flights [ ]

Points Total

[ ] (A) + (B) + (C) ◄

Beverage Total

[ ]

EXERCISE

Completed Exercise Routine

3 x 1 Min / Exercise 1 [ ] [ ] [ ]

3 x 1 Min / Exercise 2 [ ] [ ] [ ]

3 x 1 Min / Exercise 3 [ ] [ ] [ ]

Feeling / Mood Emojis

BREAKFAST / MORNING

Points ✓

LUNCH / AFTERNOON

✓

DINNER / EVENING

✓

Morning: Points

A

Afternoon: Points

B

Evening: Points

C

DATE: / / Bed [:] Awake [:] Hours [ ]

NOTES

....
....
....
....

Today I am grateful for:
....

TO DO

- [ ]
- [ ]
- [ ]
- [ ]
- [ ]

MEAL PLANNER - Tomorrows Meals Organised!

....
....
....
....

TODAYS HEALTHY HABITS - Five a day - Colour me in - Water - Fruit & Veggies

ACTIVITY

Total Steps [ ]

Total Floors / Flights [ ]

EXERCISE _____

Completed Exercise Routine

3 x 1 Min / Exercise 1 [ ] [ ] [ ]

3 x 1 Min / Exercise 2 [ ] [ ] [ ]

3 x 1 Min / Exercise 3 [ ] [ ] [ ]

Points Total

[ ] (A) + (B) + (C) ◄

Beverage Total

[ ]

Feeling / Mood Emojis

BREAKFAST / MORNING

Points ✓

LUNCH / AFTERNOON

✓

DINNER / EVENING

✓

Morning: Points

Afternoon: Points

Evening: Points

A

B

C

DATE: / / Bed [:] Awake [:] Hours [ ]

NOTES

TO DO

☐
☐
☐
☐

Today I am grateful for:

☐

MEAL PLANNER - Tomorrows Meals Organised!

TODAYS HEALTHY HABITS - Five a day - Colour me in - Water - Fruit & Veggies

ACTIVITY

Total Steps [ ]

Total Floors / Flights [ ]

EXERCISE

Completed Exercise Routine

3 x 1 Min / Exercise 1 ☐ ☐ ☐

3 x 1 Min / Exercise 2 ☐ ☐ ☐

3 x 1 Min / Exercise 3 ☐ ☐ ☐

Points Total

[ ] (A) + (B) + (C) ◄

Beverage Total

[ ]

Feeling / Mood Emojis

BREAKFAST / MORNING

Points

LUNCH / AFTERNOON

DINNER / EVENING

Morning: Points

Afternoon: Points

Evening: Points

A

B

C

DATE: / /   Bed [:] Awake [:] Hours [ ]

NOTES

TO DO

- [ ]
- [ ]
- [ ]
- [ ]
- [ ]

Today I am grateful for:

MEAL PLANNER - Tomorrows Meals Organised!

TODAYS HEALTHY HABITS - Five a day - Colour me in - Water - Fruit & Veggies

ACTIVITY

Total Steps [ ]

Total Floors / Flights [ ]

EXERCISE

Completed Exercise Routine

3 x 1 Min / Exercise 1 [ ] [ ] [ ]

3 x 1 Min / Exercise 2 [ ] [ ] [ ]

3 x 1 Min / Exercise 3 [ ] [ ] [ ]

Points Total

[ ] (A) + (B) + (C)

Beverage Total

[ ]

Feeling / Mood Emojis

BREAKFAST / MORNING

Points ✓

LUNCH / AFTERNOON

✓

DINNER / EVENING

✓

Morning: Points   Afternoon: Points   Evening: Points

A   B   C

DATE: / / Bed [:] Awake [:] Hours [ ]

NOTES

TO DO

- [ ]
- [ ]
- [ ]
- [ ]
- [ ]

Today I am grateful for:

MEAL PLANNER - Tomorrows Meals Organised!

TODAYS HEALTHY HABITS - Five a day - Colour me in - Water - Fruit & Veggies

ACTIVITY

Total Steps [ ]

Total Floors / Flights [ ]

EXERCISE

Completed Exercise Routine

3 x 1 Min / Exercise 1 [ ] [ ] [ ]

3 x 1 Min / Exercise 2 [ ] [ ] [ ]

3 x 1 Min / Exercise 3 [ ] [ ] [ ]

Points Total

[ ] (A) + (B) + (C) ◄

Beverage Total

[ ]

Feeling / Mood Emojis

BREAKFAST / MORNING

Points ✓

LUNCH / AFTERNOON

✓

DINNER / EVENING

✓

Morning: Points

Afternoon: Points

Evening: Points

A

B

C

DATE: /   /   Bed [:   ]   Awake [:   ]   Hours [   ]

NOTES

Today I am grateful for:

TO DO

- [ ]
- [ ]
- [ ]
- [ ]
- [ ]

MEAL PLANNER - Tomorrows Meals Organised!

TODAYS HEALTHY HABITS - Five a day - Colour me in - Water - Fruit & Veggies

ACTIVITY

Total Steps [   ]

Total Floors / Flights [   ]

EXERCISE

Completed Exercise Routine

3 x 1 Min / Exercise 1   [ ] [ ] [ ]

3 x 1 Min / Exercise 2   [ ] [ ] [ ]

3 x 1 Min / Exercise 3   [ ] [ ] [ ]

Points Total

[   ]   (A) + (B) + (C)

Beverage Total

[   ]   ☑

Feeling / Mood Emojis

☺ 😐 😲 ☹

BREAKFAST / MORNING

Points ✓

LUNCH / AFTERNOON

✓

DINNER / EVENING

✓

Morning: Points

A

Afternoon: Points

B

Evening: Points

C

DATE: / / Bed [:] Awake [:] Hours [ ]

NOTES

TO DO

☐
☐
☐
☐

Today I am grateful for: ☐

MEAL PLANNER - Tomorrows Meals Organised!

TODAYS HEALTHY HABITS - Five a day - Colour me in - Water - Fruit & Veggies

ACTIVITY

Total Steps [ ]

Total Floors / Flights [ ]

EXERCISE

Completed Exercise Routine

3 x 1 Min / Exercise 1 ☐ ☐ ☐

3 x 1 Min / Exercise 2 ☐ ☐ ☐

3 x 1 Min / Exercise 3 ☐ ☐ ☐

Points Total

[ ] (A) + (B) + (C) ◄

Beverage Total

[ ]

Feeling / Mood Emojis

BREAKFAST / MORNING

Points ✓

LUNCH / AFTERNOON

✓

DINNER / EVENING

✓

Morning: Points   Afternoon: Points   Evening: Points

A [____]   **B** [____]   **C** [____]

DATE: / / Bed ⬚ : ⬚ Awake ⬚ : ⬚ Hours ⬚

NOTES

TO DO

☐
☐
☐
☐
Today I am grateful for:
☐

MEAL PLANNER - Tomorrows Meals Organised!

TODAYS HEALTHY HABITS - Five a day - Colour me in - Water - Fruit & Veggies

ACTIVITY

Total Steps ⬚

Total Floors / Flights ⬚

EXERCISE

Completed Exercise Routine

3 x 1 Min / Exercise 1 ☐ ☐ ☐

3 x 1 Min / Exercise 2 ☐ ☐ ☐

3 x 1 Min / Exercise 3 ☐ ☐ ☐

Points Total

⬚ (A) + (B) + (C) ◄

Beverage Total

⬚ ☑

Feeling / Mood Emojis

☺ 😐 😮 ☹

BREAKFAST / MORNING

Points ✓

LUNCH / AFTERNOON

✓

DINNER / EVENING

✓

Morning: Points

Afternoon: Points

Evening: Points

A

B

C

DATE: / / Bed [:] Awake [:] Hours [ ]

NOTES

Today I am grateful for:

TO DO

☐
☐
☐
☐
☐

MEAL PLANNER - Tomorrows Meals Organised!

TODAYS HEALTHY HABITS - Five a day - Colour me in - Water - Fruit & Veggies

ACTIVITY

Total Steps [ ]

Total Floors / Flights [ ]

EXERCISE

Completed Exercise Routine

3 x 1 Min / Exercise 1 ☐ ☐ ☐

3 x 1 Min / Exercise 2 ☐ ☐ ☐

3 x 1 Min / Exercise 3 ☐ ☐ ☐

Points Total

[ ] (A) + (B) + (C) ◄

Beverage Total

[ ] ☑

Feeling / Mood Emojis

☺ 😐 😮 ☹

BREAKFAST / MORNING

Points ✓

LUNCH / AFTERNOON

✓

DINNER / EVENING

✓

Morning: Points   Afternoon: Points   Evening: Points

A   B   C

DATE: / /   Bed [:]   Awake [:]   Hours [ ]

NOTES

Today I am grateful for:

TO DO

☐
☐
☐
☐
☐

MEAL PLANNER - Tomorrows Meals Organised!

TODAYS HEALTHY HABITS - Five a day - Colour me in - Water - Fruit & Veggies

ACTIVITY

Total Steps [ ]

Total Floors / Flights [ ]

EXERCISE

Completed Exercise Routine

3 x 1 Min / Exercise 1 ☐ ☐ ☐

3 x 1 Min / Exercise 2 ☐ ☐ ☐

3 x 1 Min / Exercise 3 ☐ ☐ ☐

Points Total

[ ] (A) + (B) + (C) ◄

Beverage Total

[ ] ☑

Feeling / Mood Emojis

☺ 😐 😮 ☹

BREAKFAST / MORNING

Points ✓

LUNCH / AFTERNOON

✓

DINNER / EVENING

✓

Morning: Points   Afternoon: Points   Evening: Points

● A [   ]   B [   ]   C [   ]

DATE: / / Bed [:] Awake [:] Hours [ ]

NOTES

TO DO

☐
☐
☐
☐

Today I am grateful for:

☐

MEAL PLANNER - Tomorrows Meals Organised!

TODAYS HEALTHY HABITS - Five a day - Colour me in - Water - Fruit & Veggies

ACTIVITY

Total Steps [ ]

Total Floors / Flights [ ]

EXERCISE

Completed Exercise Routine

3 x 1 Min / Exercise 1 [ ] [ ] [ ]

3 x 1 Min / Exercise 2 [ ] [ ] [ ]

3 x 1 Min / Exercise 3 [ ] [ ] [ ]

Points Total

[ ] (A) + (B) + (C) ◄

Beverage Total

[ ] ☑

Feeling / Mood Emojis

☺ 😐 😮 ☹

BREAKFAST / MORNING

Points ✓

LUNCH / AFTERNOON

✓

DINNER / EVENING

✓

Morning: Points   Afternoon: Points   Evening: Points

A   B   C

DATE: /   /   Bed [:]   Awake [:]   Hours [ ]

NOTES

Today I am grateful for:

TO DO

☐
☐
☐
☐
☐

MEAL PLANNER - Tomorrows Meals Organised!

TODAYS HEALTHY HABITS - Five a day - Colour me in - Water - Fruit & Veggies

ACTIVITY

Total Steps [ ]

Total Floors / Flights [ ]

EXERCISE

Completed Exercise Routine

3 x 1 Min / Exercise 1   ☐ ☐ ☐

3 x 1 Min / Exercise 2   ☐ ☐ ☐

3 x 1 Min / Exercise 3   ☐ ☐ ☐

Points Total

[ ]   (A) + (B) + (C) ←

Beverage Total

[ ]   ☑ ←

Feeling / Mood Emojis

☺ 😐 😮 ☹

BREAKFAST / MORNING

Points

LUNCH / AFTERNOON

DINNER / EVENING

Morning: Points

Afternoon: Points

Evening: Points

A

B

C

DATE: / / Bed [:] Awake [:] Hours [ ]

NOTES

TO DO

☐
☐
☐
☐

Today I am grateful for:

☐

MEAL PLANNER - Tomorrows Meals Organised!

TODAYS HEALTHY HABITS - Five a day - Colour me in - Water - Fruit & Veggies

ACTIVITY

Total Steps [ ]

Total Floors / Flights [ ]

EXERCISE

Completed Exercise Routine

3 x 1 Min / Exercise 1 ☐ ☐ ☐

3 x 1 Min / Exercise 2 ☐ ☐ ☐

3 x 1 Min / Exercise 3 ☐ ☐ ☐

Points Total

[ ] (A) + (B) + (C) ◄

Beverage Total

[ ] ☑

Feeling / Mood Emojis

☺ 😐 😦 ☹

BREAKFAST / MORNING

Points ✓

LUNCH / AFTERNOON

✓

DINNER / EVENING

✓

Morning: Points

A

Afternoon: Points

B

Evening: Points

C

DATE: / / Bed [:] Awake [:] Hours [ ]

NOTES

TO DO

☐
☐
☐
☐
☐

Today I am grateful for:

MEAL PLANNER - Tomorrows Meals Organised!

TODAYS HEALTHY HABITS - Five a day - Colour me in - Water - Fruit & Veggies

ACTIVITY

Total Steps [ ]

Total Floors / Flights [ ]

EXERCISE

Completed Exercise Routine

3 x 1 Min / Exercise 1 ☐ ☐ ☐

3 x 1 Min / Exercise 2 ☐ ☐ ☐

3 x 1 Min / Exercise 3 ☐ ☐ ☐

Points Total

[ ] (A) + (B) + (C)

Beverage Total

[ ]

Feeling / Mood Emojis

BREAKFAST / MORNING

Points ✓

LUNCH / AFTERNOON

✓

DINNER / EVENING

✓

Morning: Points	Afternoon: Points	Evening: Points
A	B	C

DATE: / / Bed [:] Awake [:] Hours [ ]

NOTES

TO DO

☐
☐
☐
☐
☐

Today I am grateful for:

MEAL PLANNER - Tomorrows Meals Organised!

TODAYS HEALTHY HABITS - Five a day - Colour me in - Water - Fruit & Veggies

ACTIVITY

Total Steps [ ]

Total Floors / Flights [ ]

EXERCISE

Completed Exercise Routine

3 x 1 Min / Exercise 1 ☐ ☐ ☐

3 x 1 Min / Exercise 2 ☐ ☐ ☐

3 x 1 Min / Exercise 3 ☐ ☐ ☐

Points Total

[ ] (A) + (B) + (C) ◄

Beverage Total

[ ] ☑ ◄

Feeling / Mood Emojis

☺ 😐 😮 ☹

BREAKFAST / MORNING

Points ✓

LUNCH / AFTERNOON

✓

DINNER / EVENING

✓

Morning: Points   Afternoon: Points   Evening: Points

A   **B**   **C**

DATE: / /   Bed [:]   Awake [:]   Hours [ ]

NOTES

....
....
....
....

Today I am grateful for:
....

TO DO

☐
☐
☐
☐
☐

MEAL PLANNER - Tomorrows Meals Organised!

....
....
....
....
....

TODAYS HEALTHY HABITS - Five a day - Colour me in - Water - Fruit & Veggies

---

ACTIVITY

Total Steps [ ]

Total Floors / Flights [ ]

EXERCISE ————————————

Completed Exercise Routine

3 x 1 Min / Exercise 1   ☐ ☐ ☐

3 x 1 Min / Exercise 2   ☐ ☐ ☐

3 x 1 Min / Exercise 3   ☐ ☐ ☐

Points Total

[ ]   (A) + (B) + (C) ◄

Beverage Total

[ ]   ☑

Feeling / Mood Emojis

☺ 😐 😮 ☹

BREAKFAST / MORNING

Points ✔

LUNCH / AFTERNOON

✔

DINNER / EVENING

✔

Morning: Points

Afternoon: Points

Evening: Points

A

B

C

DATE: / /   Bed [:]   Awake [:]   Hours [ ]

NOTES

Today I am grateful for:

TO DO

- [ ]
- [ ]
- [ ]
- [ ]
- [ ]

MEAL PLANNER - Tomorrows Meals Organised!

TODAYS HEALTHY HABITS - Five a day - Colour me in - Water - Fruit & Veggies

ACTIVITY

Total Steps [ ]

Total Floors / Flights [ ]

EXERCISE

Completed Exercise Routine

3 x 1 Min / Exercise 1 [ ] [ ] [ ]

3 x 1 Min / Exercise 2 [ ] [ ] [ ]

3 x 1 Min / Exercise 3 [ ] [ ] [ ]

Points Total

[ ] (A) + (B) + (C)

Beverage Total

[ ]

Feeling / Mood Emojis

BREAKFAST / MORNING

Points ✓

LUNCH / AFTERNOON

✓

DINNER / EVENING

✓

Morning: Points

A

Afternoon: Points

B

Evening: Points

C

DATE: / /   Bed [:]   Awake [:]   Hours [ ]

NOTES

TO DO

☐
☐
☐
☐

Today I am grateful for:

☐

MEAL PLANNER - Tomorrows Meals Organised!

TODAYS HEALTHY HABITS - Five a day - Colour me in - Water - Fruit & Veggies

ACTIVITY

Total Steps [ ]

Total Floors / Flights [ ]

EXERCISE

Completed Exercise Routine

3 x 1 Min / Exercise 1   ☐ ☐ ☐

3 x 1 Min / Exercise 2   ☐ ☐ ☐

3 x 1 Min / Exercise 3   ☐ ☐ ☐

Points Total

[ ] (A) + (B) + (C) ◀

Beverage Total

[ ] ☑

Feeling / Mood Emojis

😊 😐 😮 ☹

BREAKFAST / MORNING

Points ✓

LUNCH / AFTERNOON

✓

DINNER / EVENING

✓

Morning: Points

Afternoon: Points

Evening: Points

A

B

C

DATE: / / Bed [:] Awake [:] Hours [ ]

NOTES

TO DO

- [ ]
- [ ]
- [ ]
- [ ]
- [ ]

Today I am grateful for:

MEAL PLANNER - Tomorrows Meals Organised!

TODAYS HEALTHY HABITS - Five a day - Colour me in - Water - Fruit & Veggies

ACTIVITY

Total Steps [ ]

Total Floors / Flights [ ]

EXERCISE

Completed Exercise Routine

3 x 1 Min / Exercise 1 [ ] [ ] [ ]

3 x 1 Min / Exercise 2 [ ] [ ] [ ]

3 x 1 Min / Exercise 3 [ ] [ ] [ ]

Points Total

[ ] (A) + (B) + (C) ◄

Beverage Total

[ ] ☑

Feeling / Mood Emojis

☺ 😐 😮 ☹

BREAKFAST / MORNING

Points ✓

LUNCH / AFTERNOON

✓

DINNER / EVENING

✓

Morning: Points

Afternoon: Points

Evening: Points

A

B

C

DATE: / /   Bed [:]   Awake [:]   Hours [ ]

NOTES

TO DO

- [ ]
- [ ]
- [ ]
- [ ]
- [ ]

Today I am grateful for:

MEAL PLANNER - Tomorrows Meals Organised!

TODAYS HEALTHY HABITS - Five a day - Colour me in - Water - Fruit & Veggies

ACTIVITY

Total Steps [ ]

Total Floors / Flights [ ]

EXERCISE

Completed Exercise Routine

3 x 1 Min / Exercise 1 [ ] [ ] [ ]

3 x 1 Min / Exercise 2 [ ] [ ] [ ]

3 x 1 Min / Exercise 3 [ ] [ ] [ ]

Points Total

[ ] (A) + (B) + (C) ◄

Beverage Total

[ ]

Feeling / Mood Emojis

BREAKFAST / MORNING

Points ✓

LUNCH / AFTERNOON

✓

DINNER / EVENING

✓

Morning: Points   Afternoon: Points   Evening: Points

A   **B**   **C**

DATE: / / Bed [:] Awake [:] Hours [ ]

NOTES

Today I am grateful for:

TO DO

☐
☐
☐
☐
☐

MEAL PLANNER - Tomorrows Meals Organised!

TODAYS HEALTHY HABITS - Five a day - Colour me in - Water - Fruit & Veggies

ACTIVITY

Total Steps [ ]

Total Floors / Flights [ ]

EXERCISE

Completed Exercise Routine

3 x 1 Min / Exercise 1 ☐ ☐ ☐

3 x 1 Min / Exercise 2 ☐ ☐ ☐

3 x 1 Min / Exercise 3 ☐ ☐ ☐

Points Total

[ ] (A) + (B) + (C) ◄

Beverage Total

[ ] ☑

Feeling / Mood Emojis

☺ 😐 😮 ☹

BREAKFAST / MORNING

Points ✓

LUNCH / AFTERNOON

✓

DINNER / EVENING

✓

Morning: Points

Afternoon: Points

Evening: Points

A

B

C

DATE: / /   Bed [:]   Awake [:]   Hours [ ]

NOTES

....
....
....
....

Today I am grateful for:

TO DO

☐
☐
☐
☐
☐

MEAL PLANNER - Tomorrows Meals Organised!

TODAYS HEALTHY HABITS - Five a day - Colour me in - Water - Fruit & Veggies

ACTIVITY

Total Steps [ ]

Total Floors / Flights [ ]

EXERCISE

Completed Exercise Routine

3 x 1 Min / Exercise 1   ☐ ☐ ☐

3 x 1 Min / Exercise 2   ☐ ☐ ☐

3 x 1 Min / Exercise 3   ☐ ☐ ☐

Points Total

[ ]   (A) + (B) + (C) ◄

Beverage Total

[ ]   ☑

Feeling / Mood Emojis

☺ 😐 😮 ☹

BREAKFAST / MORNING

Points ✓

LUNCH / AFTERNOON

✓

DINNER / EVENING

✓

Morning: Points   Afternoon: Points   Evening: Points

A [   ]   B [   ]   C [   ]

DATE: / / Bed [:] Awake [:] Hours [ ]

NOTES

Today I am grateful for:

TO DO

☐
☐
☐
☐
☐

MEAL PLANNER - Tomorrows Meals Organised!

TODAYS HEALTHY HABITS - Five a day - Colour me in - Water - Fruit & Veggies

ACTIVITY

Total Steps [ ]

Total Floors / Flights [ ]

EXERCISE

Completed Exercise Routine

3 x 1 Min / Exercise 1 ☐ ☐ ☐

3 x 1 Min / Exercise 2 ☐ ☐ ☐

3 x 1 Min / Exercise 3 ☐ ☐ ☐

Points Total

[ ] (A) + (B) + (C) ◄

Beverage Total

[ ]

Feeling / Mood Emojis

BREAKFAST / MORNING

Points ✓

LUNCH / AFTERNOON

✓

DINNER / EVENING

✓

Morning: Points	Afternoon: Points	Evening: Points

A B C

DATE: / / Bed ⬚ : ⬚ Awake ⬚ : ⬚ Hours ⬚

NOTES

Today I am grateful for:

TO DO

- ☐
- ☐
- ☐
- ☐
- ☐

MEAL PLANNER - Tomorrows Meals Organised!

TODAYS HEALTHY HABITS - Five a day - Colour me in - Water - Fruit & Veggies

ACTIVITY

Total Steps ⬚

Total Floors / Flights ⬚

EXERCISE

Completed Exercise Routine

3 x 1 Min / Exercise 1 ☐ ☐ ☐

3 x 1 Min / Exercise 2 ☐ ☐ ☐

3 x 1 Min / Exercise 3 ☐ ☐ ☐

Points Total

⬚ (A) + (B) + (C) ◄

Beverage Total

⬚ ☑

Feeling / Mood Emojis

☺ 😐 😧 ☹

BREAKFAST / MORNING

Points ✓

LUNCH / AFTERNOON

✓

DINNER / EVENING

✓

Morning: Points

Afternoon: Points

Evening: Points

A

B

C

DATE: / / Bed [:] Awake [:] Hours [ ]

NOTES

TO DO
- [ ]
- [ ]
- [ ]
- [ ]

Today I am grateful for:
- [ ]

MEAL PLANNER - Tomorrows Meals Organised!

TODAYS HEALTHY HABITS - Five a day - Colour me in - Water - Fruit & Veggies

ACTIVITY

Total Steps [ ]

Total Floors / Flights [ ]

EXERCISE

Completed Exercise Routine

3 x 1 Min / Exercise 1 [ ] [ ] [ ]

3 x 1 Min / Exercise 2 [ ] [ ] [ ]

3 x 1 Min / Exercise 3 [ ] [ ] [ ]

Points Total

[ ] (A) + (B) + (C) ◀

Beverage Total

[ ]

Feeling / Mood Emojis

BREAKFAST / MORNING

Points ✓

LUNCH / AFTERNOON

✓

DINNER / EVENING

✓

Morning: Points   Afternoon: Points   Evening: Points

A   B   C

DATE: / / Bed [:] Awake [:] Hours [ ]

NOTES

TO DO

☐
☐
☐
☐
Today I am grateful for: ☐

MEAL PLANNER - Tomorrows Meals Organised!

TODAYS HEALTHY HABITS - Five a day - Colour me in - Water - Fruit & Veggies

ACTIVITY

Total Steps [ ]

Total Floors / Flights [ ]

EXERCISE

Completed Exercise Routine

3 x 1 Min / Exercise 1 ☐ ☐ ☐

3 x 1 Min / Exercise 2 ☐ ☐ ☐

3 x 1 Min / Exercise 3 ☐ ☐ ☐

Points Total

[ ] (A) + (B) + (C) ◄——

Beverage Total

[ ] ☑

Feeling / Mood Emojis

😊 😐 😮 ☹

BREAKFAST / MORNING

Points ✓

LUNCH / AFTERNOON

✓

DINNER / EVENING

✓

Morning: Points   Afternoon: Points   Evening: Points

A [   ]   B [   ]   C [   ]

DATE: / / Bed [:] Awake [:] Hours [ ]

NOTES

....
....
....
....

Today I am grateful for:
....

TO DO

- [ ]
- [ ]
- [ ]
- [ ]
- [ ]

MEAL PLANNER - Tomorrows Meals Organised!

....
....
....
....
....
....

TODAYS HEALTHY HABITS - Five a day - Colour me in - Water - Fruit & Veggies

ACTIVITY

Total Steps [ ]

Total Floors / Flights [ ]

EXERCISE

Completed Exercise Routine

3 x 1 Min / Exercise 1 [ ] [ ] [ ]

3 x 1 Min / Exercise 2 [ ] [ ] [ ]

3 x 1 Min / Exercise 3 [ ] [ ] [ ]

Points Total

[ ] (A) + (B) + (C) ◄─────

Beverage Total

[ ] ☑

Feeling / Mood Emojis

☺ 😐 😮 ☹

BREAKFAST / MORNING

Points

LUNCH / AFTERNOON

DINNER / EVENING

Morning: Points   Afternoon: Points   Evening: Points

A   **B**   **C**

DATE: / / Bed ☐ : ☐ Awake ☐ : ☐ Hours ☐

NOTES

TO DO

☐
☐
☐
☐

Today I am grateful for:

☐

MEAL PLANNER - Tomorrows Meals Organised!

TODAYS HEALTHY HABITS - Five a day - Colour me in - Water - Fruit & Veggies

ACTIVITY

Total Steps ☐

Total Floors / Flights ☐

Points Total

☐ (A) + (B) + (C) ◄───

Beverage Total

☐ ☑

EXERCISE

Completed Exercise Routine

3 x 1 Min / Exercise 1   ☐ ☐ ☐

3 x 1 Min / Exercise 2   ☐ ☐ ☐

3 x 1 Min / Exercise 3   ☐ ☐ ☐

Feeling / Mood Emojis

🙂 😐 😮 🙁

BREAKFAST / MORNING

Points ✔

LUNCH / AFTERNOON

✔

DINNER / EVENING

✔

Morning: Points	Afternoon: Points	Evening: Points
A	B	C

DATE: / / Bed ⬚ : ⬚ Awake ⬚ : ⬚ Hours ⬚

NOTES

TO DO

- [ ]
- [ ]
- [ ]
- [ ]
- [ ]

Today I am grateful for:

MEAL PLANNER - Tomorrows Meals Organised!

TODAYS HEALTHY HABITS - Five a day - Colour me in - Water - Fruit & Veggies

ACTIVITY

Total Steps ⬚

Total Floors / Flights ⬚

EXERCISE

Completed Exercise Routine

3 x 1 Min / Exercise 1 ⬚ ⬚ ⬚

3 x 1 Min / Exercise 2 ⬚ ⬚ ⬚

3 x 1 Min / Exercise 3 ⬚ ⬚ ⬚

Points Total

⬚ (A) + (B) + (C) ←

Beverage Total

⬚ ☑ ←

Feeling / Mood Emojis

☺ 😐 😦 ☹

BREAKFAST / MORNING

Points ✓

LUNCH / AFTERNOON

✓

DINNER / EVENING

✓

Morning: Points   Afternoon: Points   Evening: Points

A [   ]   B [   ]   C [   ]

DATE: / / Bed [:] Awake [:] Hours [ ]

NOTES

....

....

....

....

....

Today I am grateful for:

....

TO DO

- [ ]
- [ ]
- [ ]
- [ ]
- [ ]

MEAL PLANNER - Tomorrows Meals Organised!

....

....

....

....

....

....

TODAYS HEALTHY HABITS - Five a day - Colour me in - Water - Fruit & Veggies

ACTIVITY

Total Steps [ ]

Total Floors / Flights [ ]

EXERCISE

Completed Exercise Routine

3 x 1 Min / Exercise 1 [ ] [ ] [ ]

3 x 1 Min / Exercise 2 [ ] [ ] [ ]

3 x 1 Min / Exercise 3 [ ] [ ] [ ]

Points Total

[ ] (A) + (B) + (C) ◄

Beverage Total

[ ] ☑

Feeling / Mood Emojis

🙂 😐 😮 🙁

BREAKFAST / MORNING

Points ✓

LUNCH / AFTERNOON

✓

DINNER / EVENING

✓

Morning: Points

A

Afternoon: Points

B

Evening: Points

C

DATE: / / Bed [:] Awake [:] Hours [ ]

NOTES

TO DO

- [ ]
- [ ]
- [ ]
- [ ]
- [ ]

Today I am grateful for:

MEAL PLANNER - Tomorrows Meals Organised!

TODAYS HEALTHY HABITS - Five a day - Colour me in - Water - Fruit & Veggies

ACTIVITY

Total Steps [ ]

Total Floors / Flights [ ]

EXERCISE

Completed Exercise Routine

3 x 1 Min / Exercise 1 [ ] [ ] [ ]

3 x 1 Min / Exercise 2 [ ] [ ] [ ]

3 x 1 Min / Exercise 3 [ ] [ ] [ ]

Points Total

[ ] (A) + (B) + (C) ◄

Beverage Total

[ ] ☑

Feeling / Mood Emojis

BREAKFAST / MORNING

Points ✔

LUNCH / AFTERNOON

✔

DINNER / EVENING

✔

Morning: Points   Afternoon: Points   Evening: Points

A   B   C

DATE: / / Bed [:] Awake [:] Hours [ ]

NOTES

....

....

....

....

Today I am grateful for: ....

TO DO

☐
☐
☐
☐
☐

MEAL PLANNER - Tomorrows Meals Organised!

....

....

....

....

....

TODAYS HEALTHY HABITS - Five a day - Colour me in - Water - Fruit & Veggies

ACTIVITY

Total Steps [ ]

Total Floors / Flights [ ]

EXERCISE

Completed Exercise Routine

3 x 1 Min / Exercise 1 ☐ ☐ ☐

3 x 1 Min / Exercise 2 ☐ ☐ ☐

3 x 1 Min / Exercise 3 ☐ ☐ ☐

Points Total

[ ] (A) + (B) + (C) ◄

Beverage Total

[ ]

Feeling / Mood Emojis

BREAKFAST / MORNING

Points ✓

LUNCH / AFTERNOON

✓

DINNER / EVENING

✓

Morning: Points   Afternoon: Points   Evening: Points

A ☐   B ☐   C ☐

DATE: / / Bed [:] Awake [:] Hours [ ]

NOTES

TO DO

- [ ]
- [ ]
- [ ]
- [ ]
- [ ]

Today I am grateful for:

MEAL PLANNER - Tomorrows Meals Organised!

TODAYS HEALTHY HABITS - Five a day - Colour me in - Water - Fruit & Veggies

ACTIVITY

Total Steps [ ]

Total Floors / Flights [ ]

EXERCISE

Completed Exercise Routine

3 x 1 Min / Exercise 1 [ ] [ ] [ ]

3 x 1 Min / Exercise 2 [ ] [ ] [ ]

3 x 1 Min / Exercise 3 [ ] [ ] [ ]

Points Total

[ ] (A) + (B) + (C) ←

Beverage Total

[ ] ☑

Feeling / Mood Emojis

🙂 😐 😮 ☹

BREAKFAST / MORNING

Points ✓

LUNCH / AFTERNOON

✓

DINNER / EVENING

✓

Morning: Points   Afternoon: Points   Evening: Points

A   B   C

DATE: / / Bed [:] Awake [:] Hours [ ]

NOTES

TO DO

- [ ]
- [ ]
- [ ]
- [ ]
- [ ]

Today I am grateful for:

MEAL PLANNER - Tomorrows Meals Organised!

TODAYS HEALTHY HABITS - Five a day - Colour me in - Water - Fruit & Veggies

[5 water glasses] [5 apples] [5 carrots]

ACTIVITY

Total Steps [ ]

Total Floors / Flights [ ]

EXERCISE

Completed Exercise Routine

3 x 1 Min / Exercise 1 [ ] [ ] [ ]

3 x 1 Min / Exercise 2 [ ] [ ] [ ]

3 x 1 Min / Exercise 3 [ ] [ ] [ ]

Points Total

[ ] (A) + (B) + (C) ◄

Beverage Total

[ ] [✓ cup]

Feeling / Mood Emojis

☺ 😐 😮 ☹

BREAKFAST / MORNING

Points

LUNCH / AFTERNOON

DINNER / EVENING

Morning: Points   Afternoon: Points   Evening: Points

A   B   C

DATE: / / Bed [:] Awake [:] Hours [ ]

NOTES

TO DO

- [ ]
- [ ]
- [ ]
- [ ]
- [ ]

Today I am grateful for:

MEAL PLANNER - Tomorrows Meals Organised!

TODAYS HEALTHY HABITS - Five a day - Colour me in - Water - Fruit & Veggies

ACTIVITY

Total Steps [ ]

Total Floors / Flights [ ]

EXERCISE

Completed Exercise Routine

3 x 1 Min / Exercise 1 [ ] [ ] [ ]

3 x 1 Min / Exercise 2 [ ] [ ] [ ]

3 x 1 Min / Exercise 3 [ ] [ ] [ ]

Points Total

[ ] (A) + (B) + (C) ◄

Beverage Total

[ ]

Feeling / Mood Emojis

BREAKFAST / MORNING

Points ✓

LUNCH / AFTERNOON

✓

DINNER / EVENING

✓

Morning: Points   Afternoon: Points   Evening: Points

A [   ]   B [   ]   C [   ]

DATE: / / Bed [:] Awake [:] Hours [ ]

NOTES

....
....
....
....

Today I am grateful for:

TO DO

☐
☐
☐
☐
☐

MEAL PLANNER - Tomorrows Meals Organised!

....
....
....
....
....

TODAYS HEALTHY HABITS - Five a day - Colour me in - Water - Fruit & Veggies

ACTIVITY

Total Steps [ ]

Total Floors / Flights [ ]

EXERCISE

Completed Exercise Routine

3 x 1 Min / Exercise 1 ☐ ☐ ☐

3 x 1 Min / Exercise 2 ☐ ☐ ☐

3 x 1 Min / Exercise 3 ☐ ☐ ☐

Points Total

[ ] (A) + (B) + (C) ◄

Beverage Total

[ ] ☑

Feeling / Mood Emojis

☺ 😐 😮 ☹

BREAKFAST / MORNING

Points ✓

LUNCH / AFTERNOON

✓

DINNER / EVENING

✓

Morning: Points   Afternoon: Points   Evening: Points

A   **B**   **C**

DATE: /   /   Bed [:]   Awake [:]   Hours [   ]

NOTES

....

....

....

....

Today I am grateful for:

TO DO

- [ ]
- [ ]
- [ ]
- [ ]
- [ ]

MEAL PLANNER - Tomorrows Meals Organised!

....

....

....

....

TODAYS HEALTHY HABITS - Five a day - Colour me in - Water - Fruit & Veggies

ACTIVITY

Total Steps [   ]

Total Floors / Flights [   ]

EXERCISE

Completed Exercise Routine

3 x 1 Min / Exercise 1   [ ] [ ] [ ]

3 x 1 Min / Exercise 2   [ ] [ ] [ ]

3 x 1 Min / Exercise 3   [ ] [ ] [ ]

Points Total

[   ]   (A) + (B) + (C) ←

Beverage Total

[   ]

Feeling / Mood Emojis

BREAKFAST / MORNING

Points

LUNCH / AFTERNOON

DINNER / EVENING

Morning: Points

A

Afternoon: Points

B

Evening: Points

C

DATE: / / Bed [:] Awake [:] Hours [ ]

NOTES

TO DO

☐
☐
☐
☐
Today I am grateful for: ☐

MEAL PLANNER - Tomorrows Meals Organised!

TODAYS HEALTHY HABITS - Five a day - Colour me in - Water - Fruit & Veggies

ACTIVITY

Total Steps [ ]

Total Floors / Flights [ ]

EXERCISE

Completed Exercise Routine

3 x 1 Min / Exercise 1 ☐ ☐ ☐

3 x 1 Min / Exercise 2 ☐ ☐ ☐

3 x 1 Min / Exercise 3 ☐ ☐ ☐

Points Total

[ ] (A) + (B) + (C) ◄

Beverage Total

[ ] ☑

Feeling / Mood Emojis

BREAKFAST / MORNING

Points ✓

LUNCH / AFTERNOON

✓

DINNER / EVENING

✓

Morning: Points   Afternoon: Points   Evening: Points

A   B   C

Made in the USA
Middletown, DE
31 December 2018